Copyright © 2022
Published by
Amanzi Books

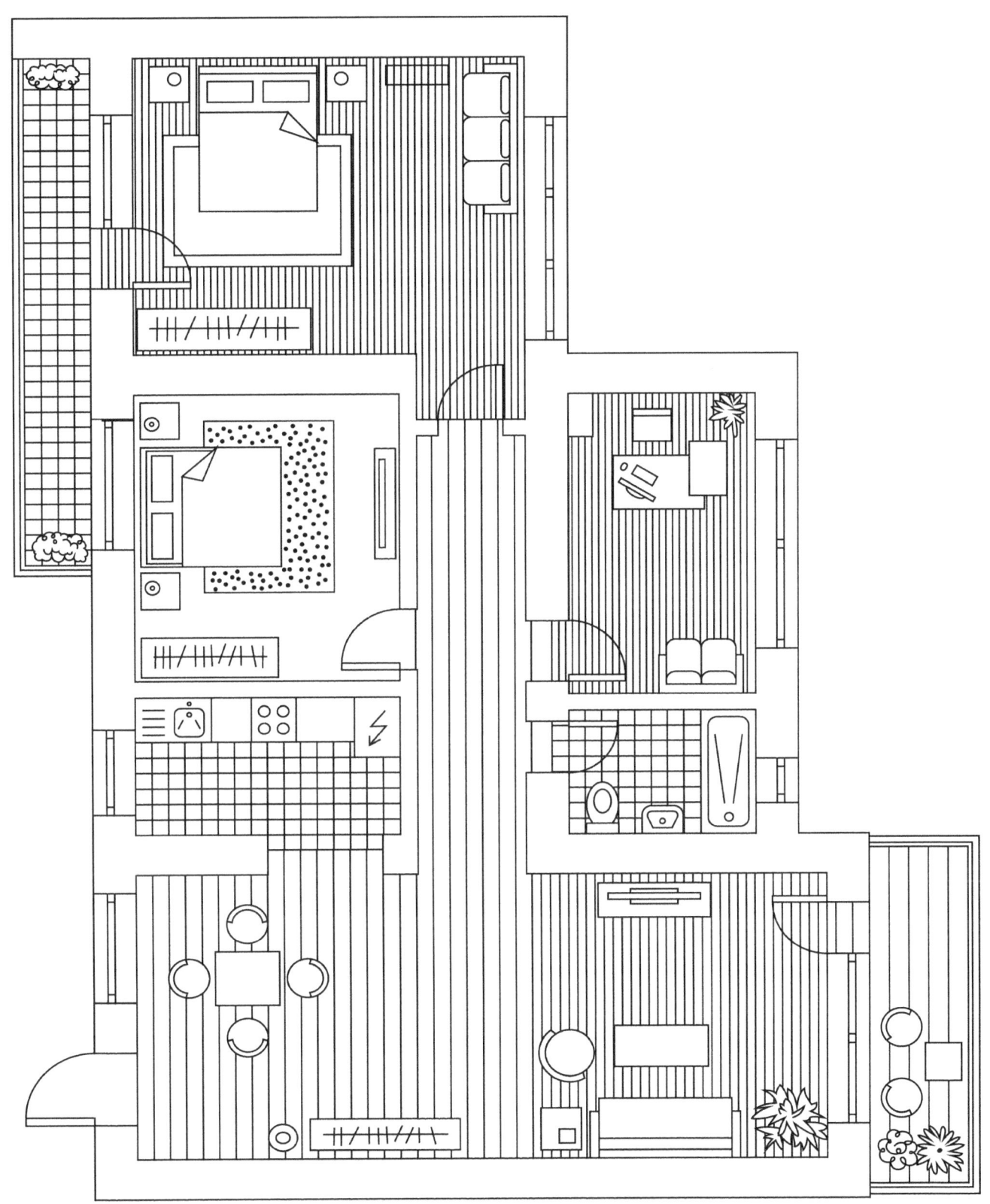

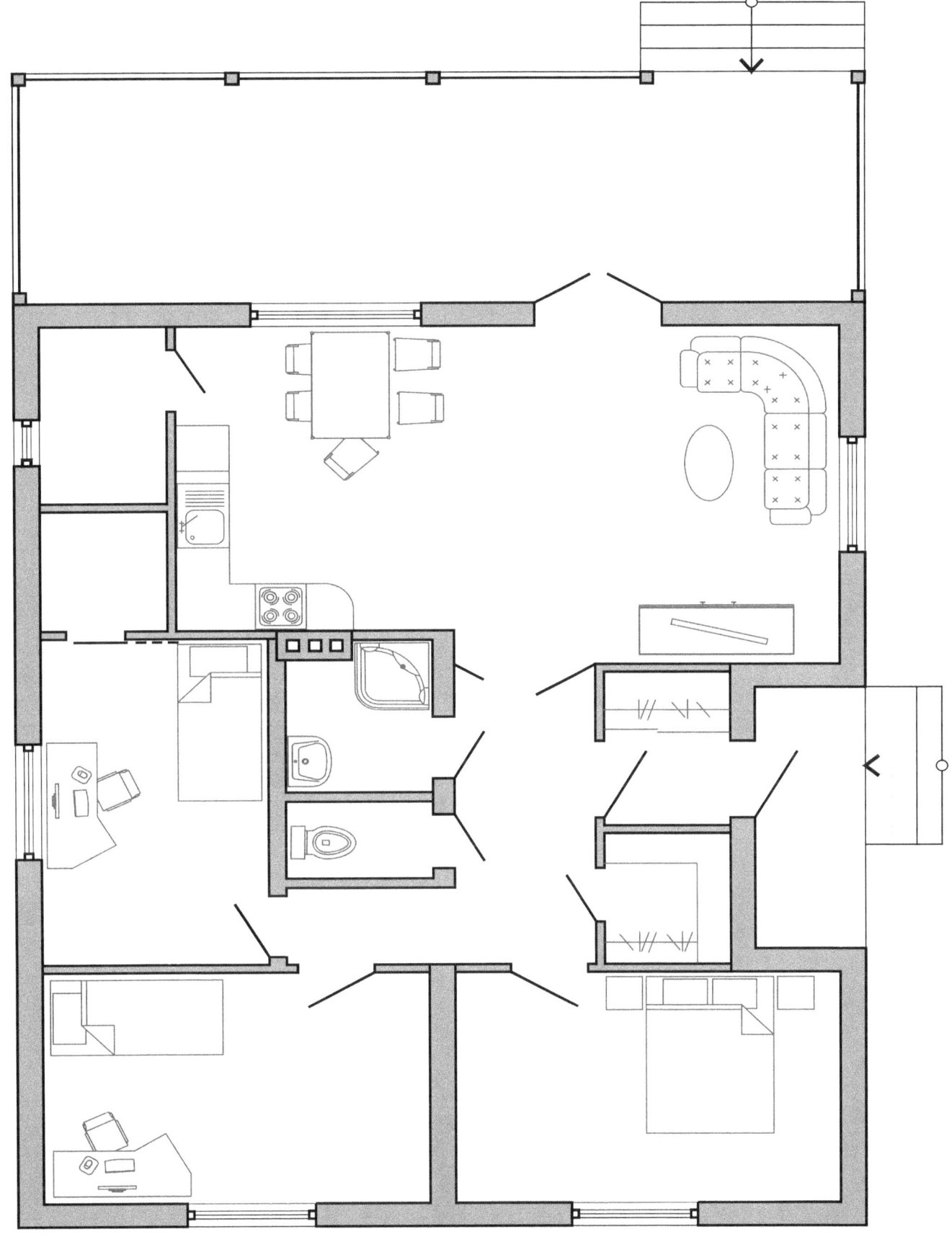

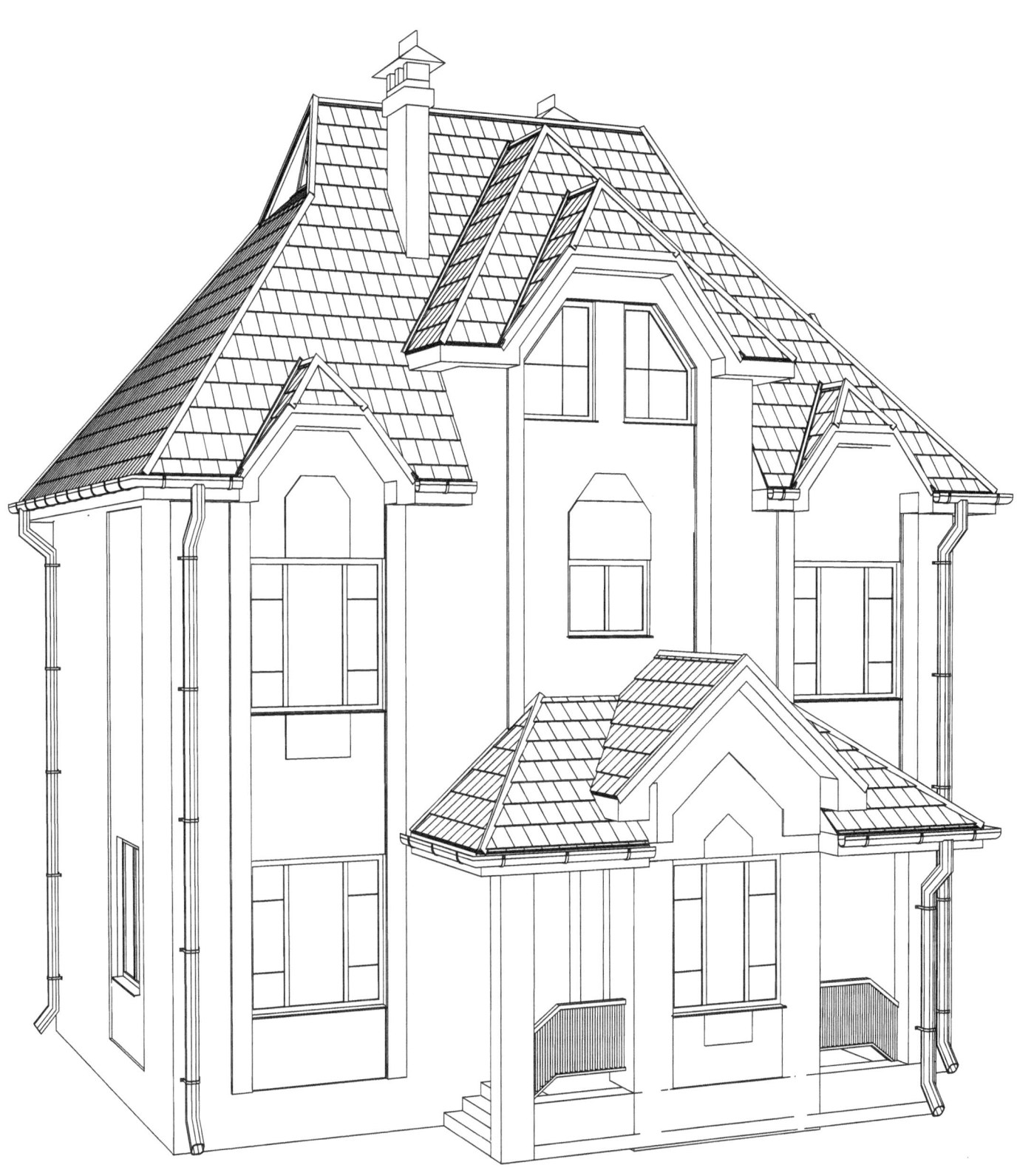

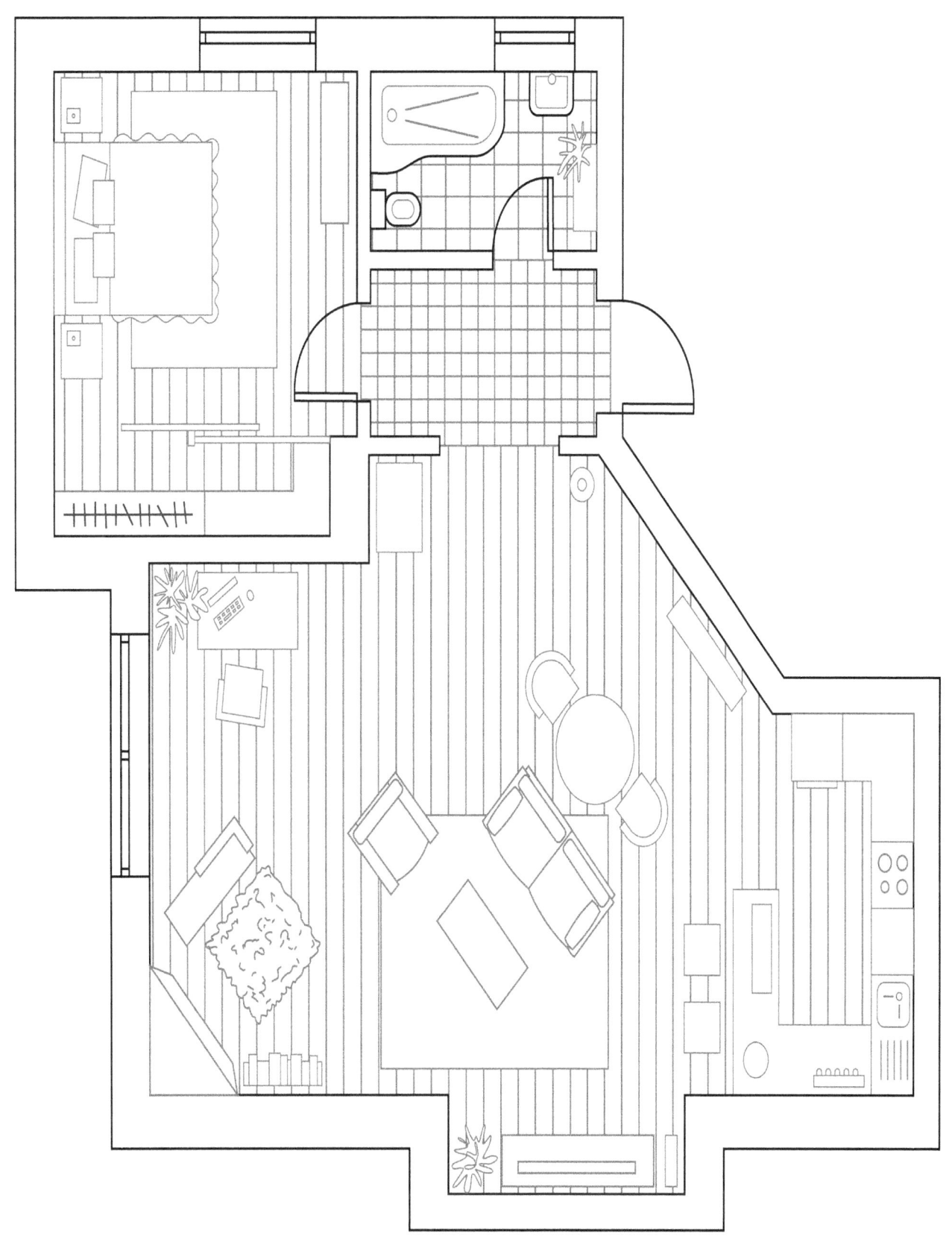

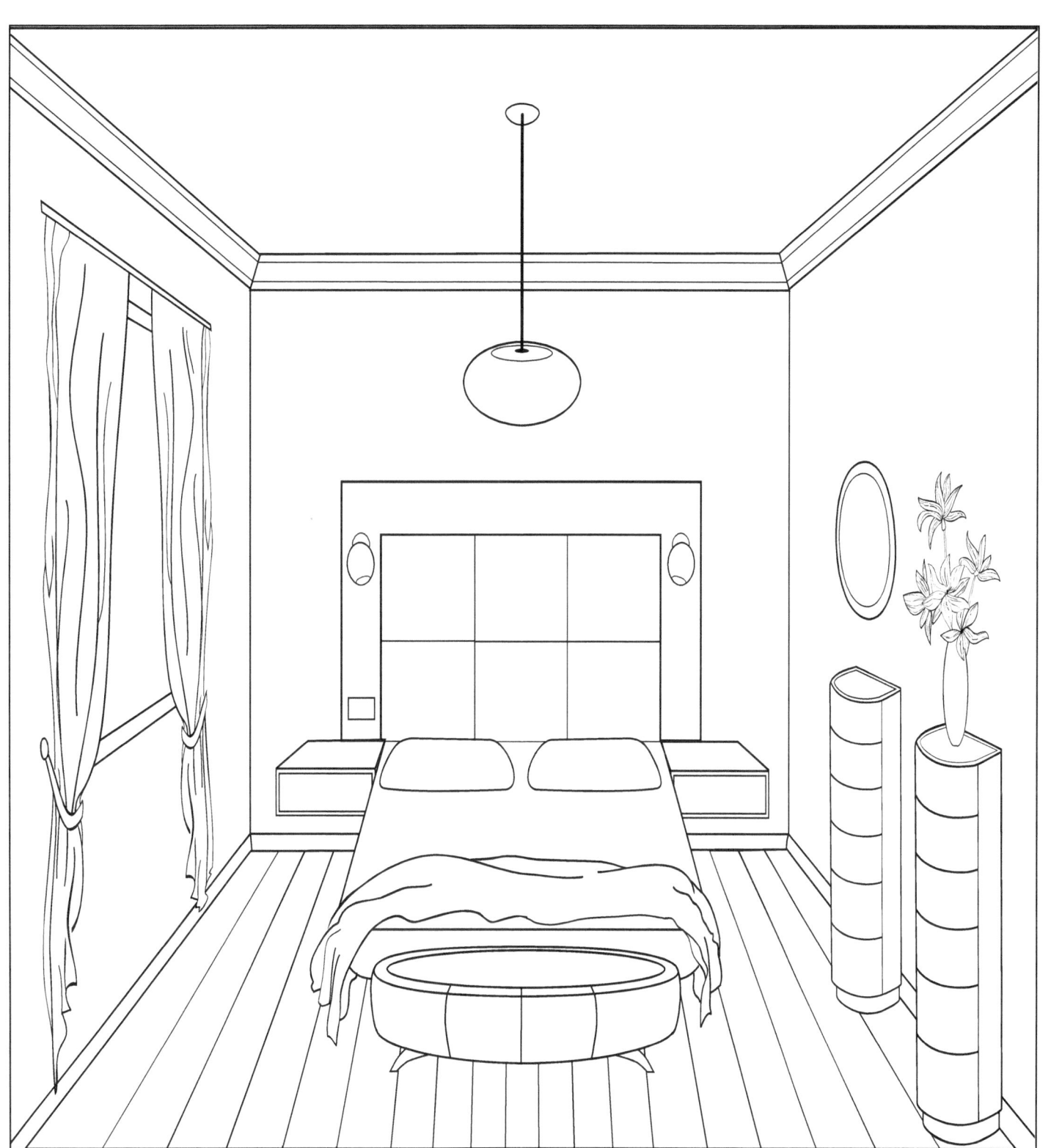

Thank you for your purchase.
Hope you enjoyed coloring!

Please rate this book ☺

www.ingramcontent.com/pod-product-compliance
Lightning Source LLC
LaVergne TN
LVHW060212080526
838202LV00052B/4263